Great Journeys Across Earth

MAGELLAN'S VOYAGE AROUND THE WORLD

Cath Senker

Heinemann
LIBRARY

www.heinemann.co.uk/library
Visit our website to find out more information about Heinemann Library books.

To order:
☎ Phone 44 (0) 1865 888066
▤ Send a fax to 44 (0) 1865 314091
▭ Visit the Heinemann Bookshop at www.heinemann.co.uk/library to browse our catalogue and order online.

MONKEY PUZZLE MEDIA LTD

Produced for Heinemann Library by Monkey Puzzle Media Ltd Gissing's Farm, Fressingfield, Suffolk IP21 5SH, UK

Heinemann library is an imprint of Pearson Education Limited, a company incorporated in England and Wales, having its registered office at Edinburgh Gate, Harlow, Essex, CM20 2JE. Registered company number: 00872828 Heinemann is a registered trademark of Pearson Education Ltd.

Editorial: Steve Parker and Louise Galpine
Design: Patrick Nugent and Victoria Bevan
Picture Research: Lynda Lines
Production: Severine Ribierre
Originated by Modern Age
Printed and bound in China by CTPS

13 digit ISBN 978 0 431 19124 9 (hardback)
12 11 10 09 08
10 9 8 7 6 5 4 3 2 1

13 digit ISBN 978 0 431 19131 7 (paperback)
13 12 11 10 09
10 9 8 7 6 5 4 3 2

British Library Cataloguing in Publication Data
Senker, Cath
Magellan's voyage around the world. - (Great journeys across Earth)
1. Magalhaes, Fernao de, d. 1521 - Travel - Juvenile literature 2. Voyages around the world - Juvenile literature
I. Title
910.4'1'092

Acknowledgements
akg-images p. 4; Alamy pp. 16 (Visual Arts Library London), 31 (Peter Treanor); Art Archive pp. 10 (Marine Museum Lisbon/Dagli Orti), 14 (Suntory Museum of Art Tokyo/Laurie Platt Winfrey), 32 (Galleria Estense Modena/Dagli Orti), 39 (Museo Naval Madrid/Dagli Orti); Bridgeman Art Library p. 5 (Private Collection/The Stapleton Collection); Corbis pp. 18–19 (Stefano Bianchetti), 22–23 (Craig Lovell), 24 (Archivo Iconografico S.A.), 28–29 (Tony Arruza), 33 (Otto Lang), 35 (Robert Garvey), 36 (Lindsay Hebberd), 40 (Historical Picture Archive); FLPA pp. 12–13 (Hiroya Minakuchi), 20 (Ingo Arndt/ Minden Pictures); Getty Images pp. 1 (Hulton Archive), 9 (Hulton Archive), 26 (The Image Bank), 41 (Hulton Archive); Mary Evans Picture Library p. 27; Nature Picture Library p. 37 (Eric Baccega); North Wind Picture Archives p. 30; Popperfoto. com p. 15; South American Pictures p. 21 (Pedro Martinez); Still Pictures p. 6 (Sean Sprague); Topfoto pp. 8 (Roger-Viollet), 17 (Peter Smith), 34 (Roger-Viollet). Maps by Martin Darlison at Encompass Graphics.

Cover photograph of a large wave in the Pacific Ocean reproduced with permission of MPM Images (Creative Collection).

Title page picture: After months of searching, in 1520 Ferdinand Magellan discovered a sea passage linking the Atlantic Ocean to the Pacific Ocean.

Expert reader: Dr Paulette Posen, environmental research scientist at the University of East Anglia

Contents

Some words are shown in bold, **like this**. You can find out what they mean by looking in the glossary.

The Spice Islands

It was 6 November, 1521. The lookout on board the Spanish ship *Victoria* called out "Land ahoy!". Could he have finally spotted the longed-for Spice Islands?

Two days later the sailors cautiously entered the harbour. Would they be attacked by angry warriors with spears? Quite the opposite. The King of Tidore floated out to meet them on his luxury boat. "I am King Al-Mansur. Welcome to the most beautiful of the Spice Islands," he called. "I dreamed you would come! You are my guests. Relax and enjoy yourselves."

The wealth of spices

Spices such as **cloves**, **cinnamon**, **mace**, and **nutmeg** grow well in the Maluku or Molucca Islands (the modern name for the Spice Islands), in modern-day Indonesia. The climate is tropical and rainfall is plentiful. Several of the islands have volcanoes. After they erupt, the volcanic ash makes the soil rich.

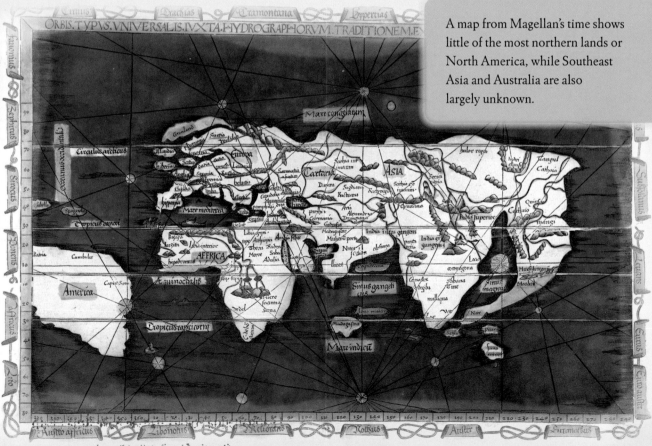

A map from Magellan's time shows little of the most northern lands or North America, while Southeast Asia and Australia are also largely unknown.

Paradise at last?

To the exhausted sailors, Tidore seemed like paradise. Here were forests of wonderful spice bushes and trees, which they had crossed the world to find. The produce of just one tree would make a sailor wealthy for life.

Juan Sebastián Elcáno, leader of the Spanish expedition, offered to trade cloth, scissors, and knives. The sailors worked quickly. They filled their ships with the precious spices and prepared to return to Spain as wealthy men.

Survival against all odds

How did the sailors manage to travel right across the world in their small ship? They had no accurate maps. They knew only parts of the main land masses, or continents – Europe, Asia, Africa, and pieces of North and South America. They had survived hunger, thirst, illness, shipwrecks, battles, and **mutiny**. Many of their companions had died from disease, torture, or drowning. Very importantly, why was their original expedition leader, Ferdinand Magellan, not with them?

Myths
Long ago there were many myths and legends about the open sea. Some people believed the world was flat, and that sailing ships could fall off the edge. Sea monsters might devour them, or mermaids tempt them overboard. In the hottest places, sailors feared that the seas might boil and destroy their ship.

Sailors believed that savage monsters lurked in distant seas, ready to devour their ships.

Planning the Voyage

Ferdinand Magellan, born in about 1480, was a Portuguese sailor who first worked for the ruler of Portugal, King Manuel. Magellan was convinced he could sail west across the Atlantic Ocean to reach the Spice Islands in the Far East, rather than make the long, dangerous journey sailing east around Africa. He begged the king to let him attempt the voyage. King Manuel did not like Magellan and refused – three times.

Spice trade

Spices were valuable to Europeans. They were used to flavour and preserve food and to make medicines. Spices were also expensive. **Islamic** *rulers controlled the Middle East and much of Asia, and would not allow European traders to cross their lands. Instead,* **Muslim** *traders bought spices and sold them on to Europeans at incredibly high prices. The Spanish and the Portuguese wanted to control the sea route to the Spice Islands and buy spices more cheaply.*

People still trade spices today, for use in flavouring delicious foods.

In 1516, Magellan went to work for King Charles I of Spain instead. He told the king he believed that the Spice Islands were in a part of the world the Spanish claimed to rule. Charles agreed to pay for the voyage and rubbed his hands in glee, at the thought of making a fortune from spices.

Portugal against Spain

Spain and Portugal were rivals. They were the most powerful countries in Europe, with the best navies. Both wanted to explore and rule countries outside Europe. Then they could control trade with them and become even wealthier. In 1512 Portuguese explorer Francisco Serrão reached the Spice Islands, claimed them for Portugal, and set up trade links. King Manuel of Portugal was furious when he heard about Magellan's expedition for the Spanish, and became determined to stop him.

The Treaty of Tordesillas

In 1494, Spain and Portugal agreed to the **Treaty** of Tordesillas. It set up an imaginary line around the globe from the **North Pole** to the **South Pole**, through the Atlantic Ocean. Spain would seize all the lands found to the west of the line, while Portugal would grab lands to the east.

This map shows how Spain and Portugal planned to divide up the world between them, according to the Treaty of Tordesillas.

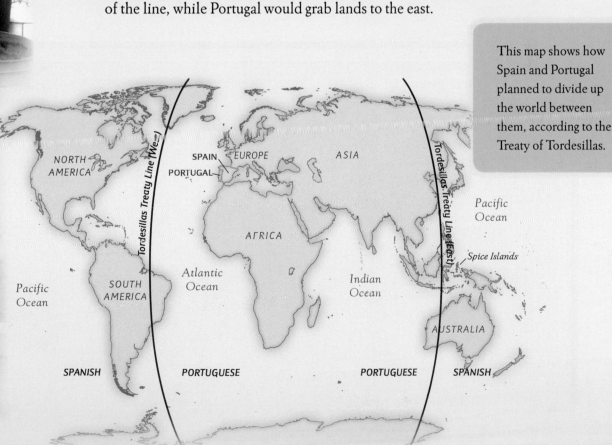

Preparing to sail

In the summer of 1519, the five ships of Magellan's fleet waited in the docks in Seville, southern Spain: *Trinidad*, *Victoria*, *Concepción*, *San Antonio*, and *Santiago*. Workers loaded them up with supplies and goods to sell. The **provisions** included wine in casks, carefully sealed to survive tossing and turning on the ocean. There were boxes of hardtack, a tasteless biscuit that sailors ate every day.

The on-board menu

The science of nutrition was little known in Magellan's time. As well as wine and hardtack, the ships carried flour for making bread, meat, cheese, figs, salted fish, chickpeas, rice, lentils, almonds, and raisins. The officers had a delicious treat – **quince jelly**. But there were no fresh vegetables or fruit, which later caused health problems for the sailors.

Seville harbour was a busy place, where ships called in for supplies before venturing out into the Atlantic Ocean.

Now Magellan had to find more than 260 sailors. A **town crier** walked the streets of Seville calling for officers, sailors, cabin boys, carpenters, and young servants or **pages**. Few Spanish sailors wanted to risk a long-distance trip under a Portuguese captain. Magellan's crew came from all over Europe and beyond. Italian crew member Antonio Pigafetta planned to write a **journal** on the voyage.

The fleet departs

Magellan captained the *Trinidad* as his flagship – the best of the fleet. The other four captains were Spanish and resented having a Portuguese leader. This would cause problems later. Meanwhile, King Manuel of Portugal tried to wreck the trip. He sent spies to Seville to frighten the captains and crews, but Magellan did not budge.

In it for profit
Cristóbal de Haro worked for the bank that lent King Charles the money for the expedition. He estimated that the trip would raise a profit of 250 per cent – it would make two and a half times as much money as the bank lent. The end of the voyage would show if he was right.

In 1513, a few years before Magellan's voyage, Spanish explorer Vasco Nuñéz de Balboa was the first European to see the Pacific Ocean, from a mountain peak in Panama, Central America.

After months of preparation, the expedition finally set sail from Seville on 10 August 1519. As the ships were taking on provisions in the Canary Islands, an urgent message warned Magellan that Portugal had sent two fleets to arrest him. In a panic, his ships left immediately.

Searching for the Strait

Fearing capture by Portuguese ships, Magellan commanded his fleet to sail as fast as possible, day and night. The ships followed the coast of Africa. Suddenly, the weather grew stormy. For two months, the fleet was constantly battered by waves. It was impossible to sleep. Boxes were broken, much food was ruined, and the crew had to eat less. Tired, hungry, and miserable, the sailors gazed in terror at the sharks circling the ship. They even caught a few to eat – but the sharks did not taste good.

Magellan is shown with his sea charts (maps) and an astrolabe (navigation instrument) on the right. His sailing ships are in the background.

Dead reckoning

*The ship's route was marked on **charts** (sea and coast maps) by working out the direction it was travelling in, and how fast. Magellan used a magnetic compass to work out the direction. To find speed, a sailor threw a piece of wood overboard, and timed how long it took for the ship to pass it. The time was kept by a sand clock – similar to an egg timer.*

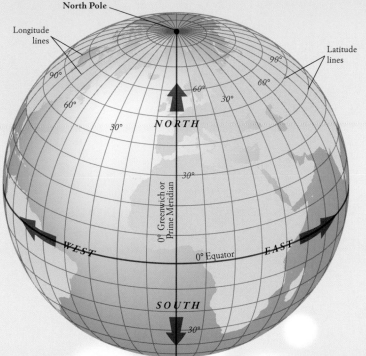

North Pole
Longitude lines
90°
60°
30°
NORTH
90°
60°
30°
60°
30°
30°
WEST
0° Greenwich or Prime Meridian
0° Equator
EAST
SOUTH
30°
Latitude lines

The Equator is an imaginary line around the middle of the Earth, midway between the poles, at 0° (degrees). Latitude measures the distance north or south from the Equator in degrees, such as 30° N or 60° S. Longitude shows the distance east or west from the Prime Meridian, which is also known as the Greenwich Meridian. This distance is also measured in degrees, such as 30° E or 60° W.

Latitude and longitude

Outside Europe, Magellan had no accurate maps. He relied on various navigation methods. His officers could work out the ship's **latitude** – its distance north or south of the **Equator**. They measured the position of the midday Sun and the **Pole Star**, which appear at different heights at different latitudes. But they did not know how to work out their **longitude** – their position east or west.

Landfall in Brazil

After the storm finally dropped, the fleet sailed southwest and in December 1519 reached Rio de Janeiro, in eastern Brazil. The sailors gratefully traded bells, knives, scissors, and mirrors with the local Guaraní people, in exchange for geese and other meats, and fresh foods such as fruit.

Men only

No women were permitted on board Magellan's ships. In Rio de Janeiro, Magellan's **pilot**, João Lopes Carvalho, met up with his Brazilian girlfriend from seven years before. He wanted to bring her and their son on board. Magellan allowed the boy to come on board, but not the mother. Before the ships left, they were searched. Several women – mostly girlfriends of crew members – were returned to shore in tears.

Duck Bay

After two weeks in Rio de Janeiro, the expedition made its way south down the coast of South America. Magellan's challenge was to discover a **strait** – a narrow sea passage that would bring the explorers from the Atlantic to the Pacific Ocean. Magellan had heard that it existed, but he had no idea where.

In January 1520, the lookout called excitedly that he had spied a **waterway**. Could this be the strait? Magellan checked, but decided it was merely a river, and the fleet continued. In fact, he was right. It was Río de la Plata, between modern-day Argentina and Uruguay.

Ducks and wolves

On 27 February the fleet reached an inlet near what is now Bahía Blanca, Argentina. Magellan named it Duck Bay. The sailors hunted the plentiful animals there, including strange birds they called "ducks", and fierce "sea wolves".

In fact the "ducks" were the tubby, flightless birds we know as penguins. The "sea wolves" were sea lions, able to use their flippers to move about on land. The sailors **gorged** themselves hungrily on the meat of these animals.

Penguins

Antonio Pigafetta said of the strange birds we now call penguins:

"These goslings are black and have feathers over their whole body... They do not fly, and they live on fish. And they were so fat that we did not pluck them but skinned them, and they have a beak like a crow's."

Winter draws in

The Southern Hemisphere is the half of the world south of the Equator. The seasons are opposite to those in the Northern Hemisphere. So by March 1520, when it would be spring in Europe, winter was approaching for Magellan and his fleet in the far south of South America. Terrible winds and storms buffeted the ships. Fortunately, on 31 March, Magellan discovered a safe harbour in Patagonia, which he named Port San Julián. The fleet stayed there for five months, sheltering from the winter storms.

Along Argentina's coast, Magellan and his crew saw – and ate – penguins. This particular kind of penguin is named in his honour as the Magellanic penguin.

Life on Board

In Port San Julián, the sailors continued work as usual. Everyone had his jobs. At the bottom of the heap were the **pages**. Some were only eight years old. They had to serve meals, scrub the decks, and do other boring tasks. Next up were the apprentices, who scrambled up the masts and **rigging** (ropes), and manned the dangerous look-out posts. Once trained, apprentices became professional sailors.

Some sailors had special jobs. Gunners kept the cannons clean and ready to fire. Carpenters repaired the boat. Caulkers sealed the spaces between the wooden planks to stop water getting in. Most of these sailors were in their teens or twenties. Magellan himself was nearly 40, very experienced, and probably the oldest person on the ship.

Sailors were constantly busy climbing the rigging, to move the sails so they could best catch the wind.

Magellan could check the first part of his route on maps. But there were no maps of his later route. He kept notes and eventually made his own maps.

Antonio Pigafetta
Pigafetta (c.1491–c.1535) was a wealthy Italian and experienced sailor, who paid to go on the expedition. He turned out to be extremely useful. He was good at learning languages and talking with the different people along the route. Pigafetta's journal described life on board ship as well as the people, places, animals, and plants he saw.

At the top were the officers. Most senior were the **pilot** who plotted the route, the **master** who was in charge of the **cargo**, and the captain who was in overall command of everyone and everything.

Mealtimes and funtimes

Sailors greatly looked forward to mealtimes as a break from hard work. The ship carried a **fire box** for cooking, with pots hung from a bar over the flames. If the weather was rough, it was too risky to light the fire. The rocking could allow the fire to spread and set light to the wooden ship. Much of the time the sailors survived on a plain diet of hardtack, bread, porridge, salted fish, and wine.

In calm waters, when supplies were plentiful, the sailors enjoyed freshly cooked, tasty meals. In their free time, they liked to play cards and dice. They enjoyed telling stories, singing, drawing, and carving models. Antonio Pigafetta recorded these and other daily events in his **journal**.

Months at sea

As time wore on, life on board ship grew harder. Everyone suffered from seasickness. There was no fresh air below decks, just horrible smells such as the stink of rotting food, especially fish. The sailors themselves were smelly.

They could wash their bodies and their clothes in sea water, but it made them itch, so they did not wash often.

The barber-surgeon

The ship's barber-surgeon did not just cut hair and shave the crew. He was a type of doctor, with a chest of herbs for treating diseases. He often pulled out sailors' rotten, painful teeth.

If a sailor suffered a badly wounded arm or leg, and it did not heal, there was a danger that the infection could spread to the rest of the body. So the barber-surgeon cut off the limb with a saw.

This 1590 painting shows an elegant European sailor, dressed in his finest clothes. Most ordinary sailors wore baggy, knee-length trousers made from wool or old sail-cloth, that soon became dirty and torn.

Pests big and small

The sailors became used to the rats and mice on board, and may even have played with them like pets. But other pests made their lives a misery. Tiny lice got into their clothes and bedding, making them scratch. Maggots and **weevils** got into the hardtack and other food. The sailors had to pick them out before eating.

At night, the swaying ship made it hard to sleep. Sailors tried to find a sheltered area of the deck and lay on a straw mattress, wrapping thick blankets around them.

Another problem was that food soon went bad or rotten. This happens because of the growth of tiny living things such as bacteria and moulds, on and in the food. The microbes form slimy threads and patches, and make the food poisonous to eat. All of this happens much faster in hot weather.

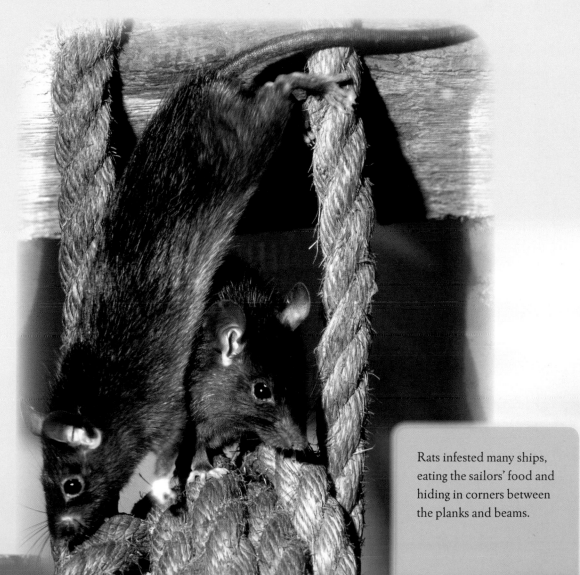

Rats infested many ships, eating the sailors' food and hiding in corners between the planks and beams.

Mutiny and Shipwreck

Port San Julián, in Patagonia, Argentina, is a natural sheltered harbour. The tall cliffs around it guard against the year-round strong winds, and there are plenty of fish to eat. During their stay there, Magellan realized that his sailors were angry and fed up. They thought they would die looking for a **strait** that did not exist. The Spanish captains were unhappy too. They hated serving under a Portuguese leader.

One night, under cover of darkness, rebel captain Juan Sebastián Elcáno seized control of the *San Antonio*. Within hours, the **mutiny** spread to the *Victoria* and the *Concepción*. The rebels prepared guns and **crossbows**, ready to fight Magellan if necessary.

Crushing the rebels

Magellan would stop at nothing to regain control. He sent loyal sailors to the *Victoria* to talk to the mutineers. The loyal sailors had hidden weapons, and stabbed rebel captain Luis de Mendoza to death. From the *Trinidad*, Magellan's men now opened fire on the *Concepción*, pounding the decks with cannonballs. Finally the last rebel captain, Juan de Cartagena, surrendered.

Magellan held an inquisition (trial) of the mutineers. He put them through gruesome torture. Cartagena and another rebel, a priest, were punished by being left behind in Port San Julián, with little hope of return home. Magellan also had the dead Mendoza's body torn apart, and the remains strung up on deck. Sailors could then see the results of disobedience.

The strappado

To strengthen his power, Magellan sometimes used a form of torture that was common for prisoners back in Spain. The victim's arms were tied behind his back and he was hung up by a rope in terrible pain – perhaps long enough to break his arms. This punishment was given to Andrés de San Martín, an **astronomer** *on the expedition, but he was not badly injured.*

The terrified crew promised to follow Magellan, after he crushed their mutiny.

Santiago shipwrecked

The mutiny over, Magellan carried on the search for the strait. Despite the wintry weather, in late April 1520 he sent the *Santiago* to look ahead. After a calm start, a huge storm broke out. The ship was tossed onto the rocky shore and broke into pieces. Incredibly, all the crew but one were able to scramble to land and survive the shipwreck.

Rescue plan

The crew managed to grab planks from the wrecked boat and build a tiny raft. It was a long and tiring process. Two brave sailors then set off back to Port San Julián. They survived a river crossing and an 11 day overland trek in icy weather, to tell Magellan of the disaster.

Surviving a shipwreck

Like many shipwrecked sailors, the Santiago crew did vital things to stay alive. They wrung out their wet clothes to stop themselves from becoming too cold, a dangerous condition known as hypothermia. They found clean drinking water from a river or collected rainwater. (Sea water makes people more thirsty because the body uses up water to filter out the salt.) They made a shelter with tree branches, and rested to save their energy until the rescue.

In South America, Magellan and his crew spotted many animals that Europeans had never seen before. These are *guanacos*, which are wild cousins of llamas.

The Tehuelche

A few weeks after the safe return of the *Santiago's* crew, Pigafetta reported a naked man on the shore of the port. He was "dancing, singing, and throwing dust on his head … He was so tall that we reached only to his waist." The sailors made friends with the man and his people, the Tehuelche. Even though King Charles had forbidden taking captives, Magellan decided to capture two "giants" for him. (They were not really giants, being about 1.8 metres or 6 feet tall, although this was taller than most Europeans of the time.)

It was common for sailors on long voyages to take captives, to prove their expedition had reached remote lands. For the captives, it was terrifying. Forced to leave their homes and families, they suffered from the harsh conditions at sea, strange foods, and new diseases.

Magellan's crew met the Tehuelche people of Patagonia, who showed them how to find local food. This photograph of the Tehuelche, taken about 100 years ago, shows them wearing *guanaco* furs.

Into the Pacific Ocean

Magellan's fleet finally set sail again on 24 August 1520. Around the end of October, the fleet rounded what is now called Cape Vírgenes, Argentina. This was not just another bay. At long last, this was the **strait** between the Atlantic and the Pacific Oceans that they had been desperately seeking. It was later named after Magellan in honour of his discovery.

The Strait of Magellan

Magellan did not realize how lucky he was to find the strait and then sail through it from east to west. The winds usually blow strongly the other way. He and his crew navigated slowly and carefully, even tasting the sea water. If it started to taste fresher, they were going inland. The saltier it was, the closer they were to the open ocean.

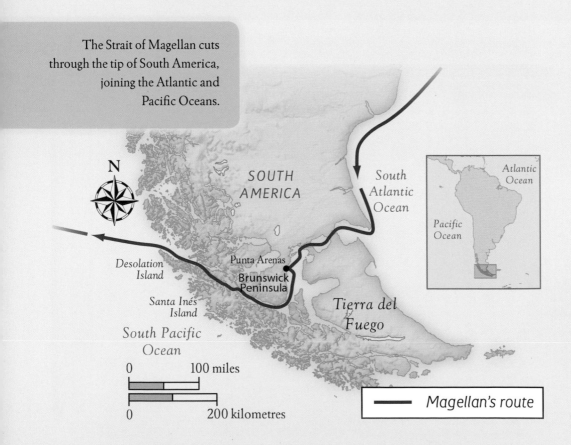

The Strait of Magellan cuts through the tip of South America, joining the Atlantic and Pacific Oceans.

One ship less

After the delight of finding the strait, disappointment followed. The crew of the *San Antonio*, afraid of the great dangers that lay ahead, refused to continue. One day in November, this ship **deserted** – disappeared and returned to Spain. On board were a Tehuelche man and most of the expedition's stores. It was a big blow to Magellan.

The remaining three ships sailed cautiously along the strait. At last, on 28 November, after 38 days, they emerged into the Pacific Ocean. Magellan was strict and tough, but he cried tears of joy when he sighted this ocean.

Tierra del Fuego

Magellan was the first European explorer to discover the land south of the strait. He named it Tierra del Fuego (Land of Fires), after the fires the local people lit for warmth. It is one of a group of islands that form the southern tip of South America.

Today, Puntas Arenas in Chile is the main town near the Strait of Magellan.

Across the Pacific

The Pacific Ocean covers one-third of Earth's surface. Magellan had no idea how large it was, and he hoped to cross it in a few weeks. His hopes turned to fears as the ships sailed endlessly on the open seas, with not a single island in sight. Magellan threw his sea **charts** overboard in a rage because "the Moluccas are not to be found in their appointed place".

The ocean deep

The Pacific is the world's largest ocean – bigger than all the other seas and oceans added together. The Mariana Trench in the northwest Pacific is the deepest place on Earth – more than 11,000 metres (36,000 feet) from the surface to the seabed.

In the Pacific Ocean, Pigafetta spotted flying fish. But this painting shows them many times bigger than their real size!

Trade winds

As Magellan's ships crossed the Pacific, steady winds pushed them in the direction of the Spice Islands. These were the Trade Winds, named because they helped trading ships. Such winds occur because of differences in air pressure. Some regions of Earth warm up faster than others. The warm air rises and cooler air moves along to replace it, as wind. The spinning of Earth also affects the wind patterns.

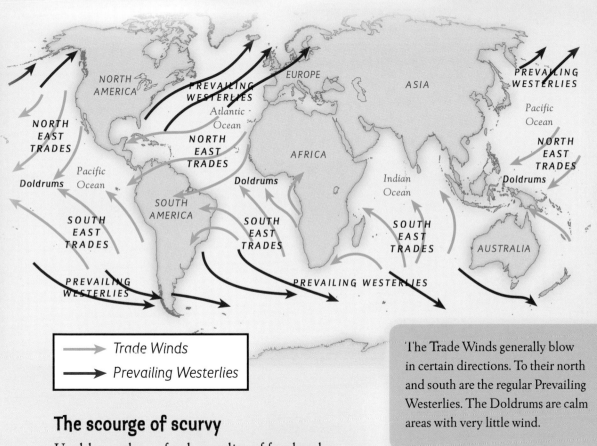

→	Trade Winds
→	Prevailing Westerlies

The Trade Winds generally blow in certain directions. To their north and south are the regular Prevailing Westerlies. The Doldrums are calm areas with very little wind.

The scourge of scurvy

Unable to take on fresh supplies of food and water, the crew endured utter misery. One captive and 29 sailors died a slow, painful death from **scurvy**, the biggest health problem on board. It made a sailor's gums swell, and his teeth fall out. His joints became stiff, and he bled under the skin. Unable to eat, he weakened and died.

Scurvy is caused by lack of vitamin C. The sailors had no fresh fruit or vegetables, the main source of vitamin C. Strangely, the officers did not suffer, although no one knew why. In fact, the delicious **quince jelly** they kept to themselves contained vitamin C.

Land at last

After 99 days at sea, the expedition finally reached Guam in the Mariana Islands on 6 March 1521. Magellan was probably the first person to cross the entire Pacific Ocean in a single voyage. It was bad luck he did not come across any of the South Pacific islands. Then he could have taken on fresh food and water and avoided the terrible deaths from scurvy.

Cannibal cure

Some men suffering from scurvy were so desperate, they were prepared to become **cannibals**. They thought that eating human organs could cure the disease. They asked their fellow sailors to bring them the innards of dead bodies of local people to eat. This "cure" would not have worked!

Navigating by nature
Pacific island people used nature to find their way. For example, they followed birds after a day's fishing at sea, because the birds were heading back to their nests on land. Pacific sailors also knew that many islands were in groups, called archipelagos. If they found one island, there were probably others nearby.

Coconut palms grow along the shores of many tropical islands. Their large leaves, wood, and coconut fruits have many uses.

The Chamorros

The surviving sailors were desperate for food. Suddenly, hundreds of native people from Guam, the Chamorros, raced out to Magellan's fleet in their light, fast canoes. They swarmed on board and took everything they could lay their hands on. Then they offered coconuts and fish to the hungry sailors. How confusing!

The Chamorros believed that all things should be shared. The Europeans did not think like this at all. When the Chamorros took Magellan's small rowing boat, the crew grew angry. They killed seven native people and burned down many of their houses. As soon as the crew found their boat, they rapidly set sail.

The canoe used by the Chamorros, called the *proa*, went so fast that it seemed to fly over the water. The bow (front) and stern (back) of a *proa* are the same, so it can change direction easily. It has two **hulls**, large and small, to prevent tipping over.

The Philippine Islands

Magellan's ships sailed on to what are now the Philippine Islands. In the middle of March 1521, they dropped anchor at Homonhon Island. Nervous after their experience with the Chamorros, this time the explorers got on well with the local people. They traded cloth, mirrors, and glassware for fruit, vegetables, meat, and coconuts with their many uses. The men suffering from **scurvy** soon recovered. When the crew showed off their weapons and armour, Magellan noticed that the Filipino people appeared terrified.

The Philippine Islands

The Philippines are a group of around 7,100 islands in Southeast Asia, northeast of Malaysia. As Magellan found, the climate is tropical, so the temperature varies little all year. Monsoon winds bring rain from the southwest during the middle of the year, and from the northeast from November to February. Violent tropical storms called typhoons regularly strike the islands, with high winds and floods.

The fleet moved through the islands, stopping at Limasawa and Cebu. In Cebu, Magellan persuaded the local ruler, Humabon, and his people to become followers of the Christian religion and swear loyalty to Spain. Humabon was happy to do this. He liked having European **allies** with powerful weapons. With Spanish support, he would be stronger than the other local rulers.

Weapons and armour
Magellan's fleet carried a huge supply of weapons to protect the crew. There were three cannons, more than 100 guns, and several tonnes of gunpowder. The crew also had **crossbows***, javelins (spears), and swords and knives for close-up fighting. They had body armour for protection, but their legs were uncovered so they could walk and run easily.*

The coconut

On the Philippine Islands, the Europeans were amazed at the many uses of the coconut. Pigafetta thought the white flesh tasted liked almonds, and the milk was very refreshing. The Filipinos made coconut oil for cooking by boiling the flesh and milk. They used the fibres from the shell-like husk to make rope for binding together their boats.

This cross, with a painted ceiling above it, is in a church built to mark the spot where Magellan landed in Cebu, in 1521. The ceiling shows the European sailors meeting local people.

Into battle

Sula, one of the rulers of Mactan Island in the Philippines, asked Magellan for support against Lapu Lapu, a rival king on the island. Lapu Lapu had refused to convert to Christianity and swear loyalty to Spain. Magellan's men had already burned down his village. This would be round two of the fight.

No chance for the leader

On 27 April 1521, Magellan and 48 men, heavily armed with swords, axes, crossbows, and guns, sailed to Mactan Island. They were confident of easy victory. On arrival, they were horrified to see the coast was very rocky. As they waded ashore, clumsy in their armour, 1,500 Filipino fighters rushed at them with loud cries. The warriors flung their poisoned arrows at the sailors' bare legs. Then the warriors saw Magellan, and hurled themselves wildly at him, stabbing and hacking, until he fell dead. Eight other sailors were killed while the rest struggled back to the ship.

The Battle of Mactan

Antonio Pigafetta described the battle in which Magellan was killed:

"They shot so many arrows at us and hurled so many bamboo spears (some of them tipped with iron) at the captain-general (Magellan), besides pointed stakes hardened with fire, stones, and mud, that we could scarcely defend ourselves."

At the Battle of Mactan in 1521, the Europeans in armour could hardly move, while the local warriors charged around freely.

Who is the hero?

For the crew of the expedition, Magellan's death was a disaster. Yet to the Filipinos, Lapu Lapu was a hero who forced the European invaders to leave. Both sides of the story are remembered today. There is a monument to Magellan at the spot where he died. Nearby is a statue of Lapu Lapu in heroic pose with a sword and shield.

The statue of Lapu Lapu on Mactan Island, Cebu, in the Philippines, celebrates his victory over the Europeans.

Enrique the slave

*Magellan's **slave** Enrique (born about 1493) probably came from Sumatra, Indonesia. Magellan had bought him on a previous trip to Malacca, Malaysia in 1512. Now Enrique had become a crew member and translator. After Magellan died, Enrique should have been freed, but the other captains refused. Enrique was so enraged, he may have betrayed the expedition at a later stage.*

Escape from Cebu

The entire crew were shocked by Magellan's death. Yet there was worse to come. On 1 May 1521 the local ruler Humabon invited them to a delicious feast. While they were happily sipping palm wine, Humabon's armed warriors ambushed them. They sprang out from among the trees and furiously attacked the visitors, killing 27 men.

Why did Humabon turn against his European allies? Some of the crew believed that Magellan's slave Enrique was to blame. Angry at not being set free, he convinced Humabon to turn against the Europeans.

The surviving sailors fled in terror. Of the 260-plus men who had set out from Seville, 115 now remained – too few to crew three ships. They burned the *Concepción* rather than risk it falling into enemy hands.

The San Antonio

*On 6 May 1521, just after Magellan's death, the San Antonio – which had **deserted** the fleet in South America – finally reached Spain. The crew told Spanish officials how Magellan had tortured and killed Spanish officers and put the expedition in danger. Would the crews of the other ships ever return to tell their side of the story?*

Expeditions of the time stopped regularly for repairs. The sailors heaved the ships onto one side in shallow water, for cleaning and mending.

Brunei and beyond

The crew now had one aim – to reach the Spice Islands alive. They stopped off a few times for fresh supplies, then left again in a hurry. Yet they could not resist the warm welcome in one place – Brunei. They were invited to ride on elephants and meet the king!

Just after leaving Brunei, the *Trinidad* ran aground. Juan Sebastián Elcáno, once a mutineer at Port San Julián, was now leading the expedition. He agreed to stop for repairs. But their troubles were far from over.

Magellan's crew would have met local people sailing around the Philippines in small boats like these *vintas*, with their colourful sails.

Wild lands of Borneo
In 1521, the King of Brunei controlled the whole of Borneo, the third largest island in the world. It has such thick rainforests and tall mountains that much of the island has never been explored. Borneo is home to rhinoceroses, elephants, deer, orang-utans, bears, crocodiles, and snakes. Today much of its wildlife is in danger due to the felling of forests for timber.

Spice Islands and Home

By October 1521, Elcáno and the two remaining ships had lost their way. In despair, the sailors threatened the crews of passing boats, shouting: "Tell us the way to the Spice Islands or we'll kill you!" Finally they captured a navigator who led them to their destination. On 6 November, at last they set eyes on the Spice Islands, or Moluccas, and jumped for joy at the riches that would soon be theirs.

The Molucca islands

There are around 1,000 islands in the Moluccas (Maluku), in modern-day Indonesia. In Magellan's time, Europeans were interested in only a few of these, such as Tidore, where **cloves**, **nutmeg**, **mace**, and other spices grew freely.

Juan Sebastián Elcáno became the new leader of the expedition after Magellan's death.

Volcanoes

Many of the Molucca Islands have volcanoes. The region is part of the "Ring of Fire", a huge curving line of volcanoes encircling almost all of the Pacific Ocean. Volcanoes occur here because of Earth's structure. The outer layer, or crust, is made from huge, rigid areas called tectonic plates, which move slowly. As the plates push and pull each other, pressure along their edges forces magma (red-hot melted rocks) from deep below, up through cracks and holes. The magma bursts out in volcanic eruptions. The biggest volcanic explosion of modern times, on the island of Krakatoa, occurred in the region in 1883.

Switching loyalty

The travellers landed on the island of Tidore on 8 November, and met the king, Al-Mansur. He was fed up with the Portuguese, who had set up trade nine years earlier. The Portuguese had demanded that the king trade with them alone, so they could have the riches of the island to themselves.

However, Al-Mansur welcomed trade with everyone. He also decided it would be useful to have Spanish **allies**. This would strengthen him against his enemies on the neighbouring island of Ternate, which was still friendly with Portugal. So Al-Mansur said he would now serve the King of Spain. Elcáno wanted to trade for spices as quickly as possible and leave before there could be any more disasters.

Nutmeg is a hard seed that is harvested and grated to make a sweet-smelling spice.

Rushed repairs

Through November, the sailors busily traded for spices. They found time to rest, enjoy the warm weather, and make friends with the local people. Then one night, Elcáno discovered that Portuguese warships were on their way to Tidore. Alarmed, he rushed to prepare the ships for departure – leaving vital repairs undone.

On a fine day in December 1521, the *Victoria* and *Trinidad* set sail. But at once the *Trinidad* started to leak. With the Portuguese in hot pursuit, there was no time to lose. The *Victoria* sailed on.

Capture of the Trinidad

In May 1522 a Portuguese fleet arrived at Tidore. Its captain, António de Brito, was furious with Al-Mansur for trading with the Spanish. He reclaimed Tidore for Portugal and made plans against the Spanish ships. How dare they travel to the Spice Islands? The Portuguese had got there first, and the islands belonged to them!

Magellan's sailors marvelled at spice bushes and trees, like these clove trees growing today in Java, Indonesia.

Wildlife in the Moluccas

The Molucca Islands are rich not only in spices, but also in wildlife, especially amazing birds. The flightless cassowary grows to an incredible 2 metres (6.5 feet) tall. The colourful greater bird of paradise is maroon with a yellow crown, and the male displays thick yellow feathers. The king cockatoo has a red tuft of feathers on its head.

Taken as slaves

Shortly after de Brito arrived at Tidore, his ships captured the *Trinidad*, which was still near the Moluccas. He forced the crew to work like **slaves**, building a Portuguese fort in the area. Few would ever return home. Meanwhile Elcáno headed back in the *Victoria*, with about 60 crew and captives. One ship, alone on the sea, would attempt the 16,000-kilometre (10,000-mile) journey back to Spain.

Dangerous deals

While Elcáno's Spanish ships were in the Moluccas, Al-Mansur was happy to be allied with Spain. Yet once the fleet had gone, he was in a dangerous situation, because neighbouring islands were allied with Portugal. When de Brito's Portuguese fleet arrived, with its powerful weapons, he had little choice but to accept Portuguese rule once more.

The islands of Southeast Asia were home to many amazing creatures the Europeans had never seen, such as this greater bird of paradise.

The last leg home

Scared of capture, Elcáno made one last stop in Timor, near northern Australia, where two men **deserted**. Then the *Victoria* ploughed across the Indian Ocean. Elcáno skilfully navigated through fierce winds to round the Cape of Good Hope, at the southern tip of Africa, in May 1522.

For two months, the small ship sailed northwest up the African coast and across the **Equator** once more, without stopping. Twenty-one more crew died an agonizing death from **scurvy**, and their bodies were tossed into the sea. Down to around 30 men, Elcáno had a tough choice. Should he continue and face almost certain death from scurvy, or risk capture on the Portuguese-owned Cape Verde Islands?

Danger at Cape Verde

Elcáno landed at Cape Verde in July. The men pretended they had got lost. They managed to fool the Portuguese and buy some rice. However, on one trip ashore, 13 men failed to return to the *Victoria*. Elcáno did not know if the missing men had been arrested, or had given themselves up to the Portuguese. Fearing their enemies would discover the truth, the *Victoria* hastily set sail.

Safe at last

On 8 September 1522, the battered ship finally returned to Seville in Spain. Of the 60 men who had left the Moluccas, just 18 starved, filthy sailors and four captives wobbled shakily on to dry land.

International Date Line

When the Victoria *arrived in the Cape Verde Islands, the sailors discovered it was Thursday, rather than Wednesday, as they believed. Yet their time-keeping had been accurate. This was the first time that people realized the need for an International Date Line. The modern International Date Line is an imaginary line running north–south in the Pacific Ocean. Crossing it from west to east means jumping back one whole day (24 hours), and from east to west, going forward one day.*

Profit from disaster

Four ships had been lost on the great round-the-world expedition. But the 381 sacks of high-quality cloves aboard the *Victoria* were enough to make a handsome profit for merchant Cristóbal de Haro. He shared his gain with the King of Spain.

This artist's version shows Elcáno and the few remaining crew finally returning to Seville. In real life they would have been dirty, with long hair and beards, and unsteady on their legs after months at sea.

An Epic Journey

King Charles of Spain soon heard news of the *Victoria*'s return. Even though Elcáno had helped to lead the **mutiny** against Magellan, Charles welcomed him as a hero for returning with a wealth of spices. Magellan's role in the voyage might have been forgotten, had Antonio Pigafetta not published his **journal**. Pigafetta claimed Magellan had always been loyal to the king.

New knowledge

Both Magellan and Elcáno helped achieve the first **circumnavigation** of the globe – a voyage all around the world and back to the start. Magellan had discovered just how big the Pacific Ocean is. Europeans realized the world was larger than they had thought – and that Earth was definitely round. The voyage gave them important new information.

This map from about 1600 shows the Strait of Magellan, named after the sailor who died on his quest.

Named in honour

*Magellan hoped to return to Spain a rich man, and even to own the islands he discovered. These would have passed to his children, to keep alive the memory of his name. But his memory lives on for another reason. In 1536 Flemish map-maker Gerardus Mercator produced a globe that named the narrow passage he had sailed through, from the Atlantic to the Pacific, as the **Strait of Magellan**. It keeps that name to this day.*

Magellan had also shown that the Americas were not part of India, as many Europeans had believed, but formed a separate continent. The explorers disproved the strange myths of earlier times. They had discovered an amazing variety of people, animals, and plants, but they had not seen monsters, mermaids, or boiling seas.

After Magellan

Now that Spain had a sea route to the Spice Islands, Charles sent several more well-equipped expeditions to take control of the trade from Portugal. But none succeeded. These failures show the great achievement of one small sailing ship and 18 men, who survived a three-year journey all around the globe – which no one had done before.

The greatest

Laurence Bergreen, prize-winning author of books about people in history, wrote in 2003:

"Although no continent or country was named after him, Magellan's expedition stands as the greatest sea voyage in the Age of Discovery."

A dramatic painting shows Magellan's discovery of the strait that would eventually bear his name.

Around the Globe

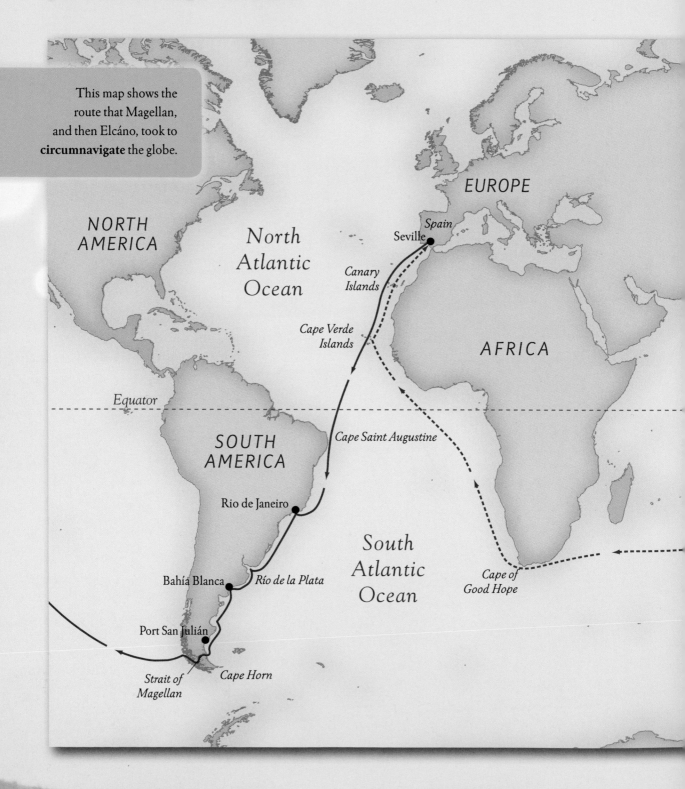

This map shows the route that Magellan, and then Elcáno, took to **circumnavigate** the globe.

NORTH
AMERICA

North
Atlantic
Ocean

EUROPE

Spain

Seville

*Canary
Islands*

*Cape Verde
Islands*

AFRICA

Equator

SOUTH
AMERICA

Cape Saint Augustine

Rio de Janeiro

South
Atlantic
Ocean

Bahía Blanca   *Río de la Plata*

*Cape of
Good Hope*

Port San Julián

*Strait of
Magellan*   *Cape Horn*

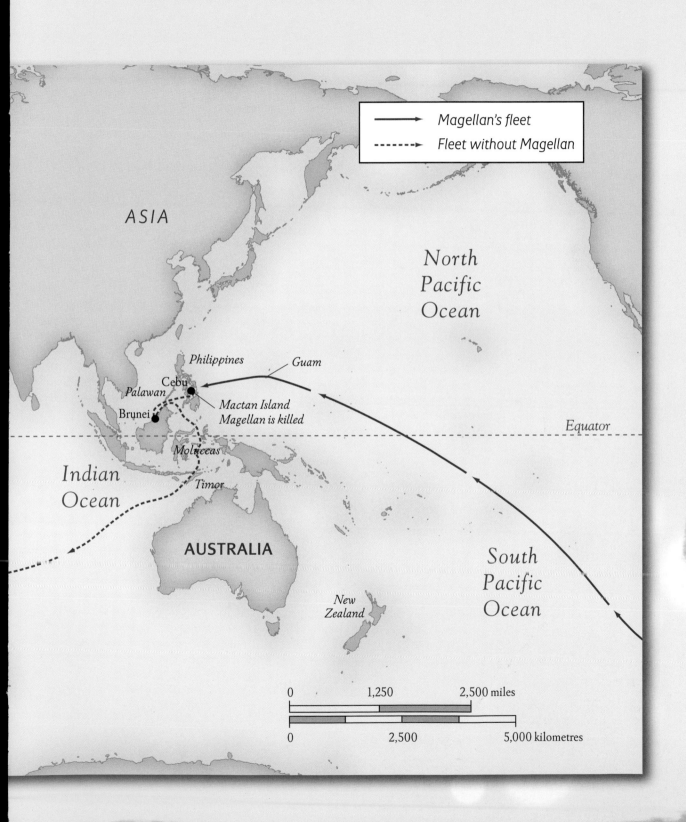

Magellan's fleet

Fleet without Magellan

ASIA

North
Pacific
Ocean

Philippines   Guam

Cebu

Palawan

Brunei   Mactan Island
                Magellan is killed

                                                        Equator

Moluccas

Indian
Ocean   Timor

            AUSTRALIA   South
                               Pacific
            New   Ocean
            Zealand

0   1,250   2,500 miles

0   2,500   5,000 kilometres

Timeline

c. 1480	Ferdinand Magellan is born in Sabrosa or Porto, in Portugal
1494	Spain and Portugal agree to the Treaty of Tordesillas, which divides newly discovered lands between the two countries
1511	Magellan fights in a battle to win control of the Malacca Strait from the Arabs
1512	Portuguese explorer Francisco Serrão reaches the Spice Islands and claims them for Portugal, as Magellan returns to Portugal
1516	Magellan stops working for King Manuel of Portugal
1517	Magellan arrives in Seville, Spain, where he goes to work for King Charles I
22 March 1518	King Charles agrees to Magellan's plan to sail west, to try and find a route to the Spice Islands
10 August 1519	Magellan's fleet of five ships sets sail from Seville, Spain
26 September 1519	The fleet visits the Canary Islands and takes on provisions
13 December 1519	The ships arrive in Rio de Janeiro, Brazil, and stop to trade
January 1520	The fleet reaches Río de la Plata, Argentina, but it is a river, rather than the strait they are seeking
31 March 1520	Magellan discovers a safe harbour in Patagonia. He names it Port San Julián and stays for the winter.
April 1520	Magellan survives a mutiny and regains control of the fleet. He sends the *Santiago* to look ahead but it is shipwrecked. The crew are rescued.
June 1520	The sailors meet the Tehuelche people of Patagonia
24 August 1520	The fleet sets sail again from Port San Julián
21 October 1520	The fleet rounds Cape Vírgenes, Argentina, and enters the strait between the Atlantic Ocean and Pacific Ocean
November 1520	The *San Antonio* deserts and sets off back to Spain

28 November 1520	Magellan's fleet emerges into the Pacific Ocean
6 March 1521	Magellan arrives in Guam in the Mariana Islands
mid-March 1521	Magellan stops at Homonhon Island in what are now the Philippines
March–April 1521	The expedition travels through the Philippines, stopping at Limasawa and Cebu
27 April 1521	Magellan's men battle the warriors of Mactan Island. Magellan and eight of his men are killed.
1 May 1521	Humabon of Cebu ambushes the Europeans and kills 27. The survivors flee in their ships.
6 May 1521	The *San Antonio*, having deserted months earlier, arrives back in Spain
October 1521	The expedition, now under the command of Juan Sebastián Elcáno, becomes lost south of the Philippines
6 November 1521	The lookout on board the *Victoria* spies land – the Spice Islands at last
8 November 1521	The expedition lands in Tidore in the Spice Islands
21 December 1521	The *Victoria* leaves Tidore, but the *Trinidad* needs further repairs
January–February 1522	Elcáno and crew stop at the island of Timor, north of Australia, where two crew members desert, then head for home
6 April 1522	The *Trinidad* leaves Tidore
May 1522	The *Victoria* rounds the Cape of Good Hope, the southern tip of Africa
13 May 1522	A Portuguese fleet arrives in Tidore and reclaims the island for Portugal. Soon afterwards, it captures the *Trinidad*.
9 July 1522	The *Victoria* reaches the Cape Verde Islands, west of modern Senegal, and stops for provisions, but hurriedly sails away
8 September 1522	The *Victoria* arrives home in Seville, completing the first ever circumnavigation of the globe
1536	Flemish map-maker Gerardus Mercator produces a globe that names the passageway at the tip of South America as the Strait of Magellan

Glossary

ally country or people that help each other, for example, defending each other against enemies

astronomer person who studies stars, planets, moons, and space

cannibal person who eats human flesh

cargo goods that are carried on a ship, usually for sale

chart map used to plot a route at sea

cinnamon sweet-smelling spice made from the dried bark of a tree from Southeast Asia

circumnavigate travel all the way around something, such as Earth

clove dried flower bud of a tree that is used as a spice

crossbow weapon made from a bow fixed on to a larger piece of wood, that fires short, heavy arrows

desert leave without permission

Equator imaginary line around the middle of Earth, halfway between the North and South Poles

fire box metal box in which a fire is lit for cooking

gorge eat a large amount very greedily

hull main outer part or shell of a ship

Islamic to do with the faith of Islam

journal account or report, like a diary, of people, places, and events

latitude distance of a place north or south of the Equator, measured in degrees

longitude distance of a place east or west of a point on Earth, measured in degrees. In modern times, longitude is measured from an imaginary line that passes from north to south through Greenwich in England.

mace outer covering of the nutmeg, which is dried as a spice

master officer on a ship who is in charge of the cargo. It also meant a person who owned a slave.

Muslim person who follows the Islamic faith

mutiny when people refuse to obey the commander's orders on board ship

North Pole point on the surface of Earth that is the furthest north

nutmeg hard, sweet-smelling seed of a tree that is grated and used as a spice

page on a ship, usually a young and inexperienced crew member who did boring jobs like cleaning

pilot person who plots the ship's route and guides the ship using navigation equipment

Pole Star star that is above the North Pole in the night sky

provisions supplies of food and drink for a long journey

quince jelly jam made from the quince, a pear-shaped fruit

rigging ropes that support the ship's masts and control the sails

scurvy disease caused by a lack of fresh fruit and vegetables in the diet

slave person who is owned by another individual and is forced to work for that individual without pay. Slavery was common in Magellan's time.

South Pole point on the surface of Earth that is the furthest south

strait narrow passage of water that links two seas or oceans

town crier person whose job was to walk through a town shouting out the news or making announcements

treaty agreement between countries

waterway river, canal, or other route for travel by water

weevil small beetle that often feeds on stored food

Further Information

Books

Bailey, Katharine. *Ferdinand Magellan: Circumnavigating the World* (Crabtree Publishing, 2006)
Includes topics such as science, life at sea, navigation, and the effects of his voyage.

Crompton, Samuel Willard. *Ferdinand Magellan and the Quest to Circle the Globe* (Chelsea House, 2005)
Magellan's voyage to try to find a passage through South America and a westward sea route to the Spice Islands.

Johnson, Vargie. *Ferdinand Magellan, the Explorer* (KiwE Publishing, 2006)
This biographical title retells the story of Magellan's voyage and looks at how it changed the world.

Kramer, Sydelle. *Who was Ferdinand Magellan?* (Grosset and Dunlap, 2004)
Includes fact boxes and a timeline to aid the readers' understanding.

Reid, Struan. *Ferdinand Magellan* (Heinemann Library, 2001)
Magellan's life story, with details of the historical and technological background to his voyage.

For reading with an adult

Bergreen, Laurence. *Over the Edge of the World* (HarperCollins, 2003)
This book is packed with exciting accounts of the voyage and how it affected the wider world.

Pigafetta, Antonio. *Magellan's Voyage Around the World* (Marsilio Publishers, 1995)
A modern edition of the original book published by Magellan's shipmate Pigafetta, who kept a journal of the voyage.

Websites

www.cs.utexas.edu/users/s2s/latest/explore1b/src/magintro.html
Interactive site that takes the user on Magellan's journey, making the choices that he had to face on the way.

http://news.bbc.co.uk/2/hi/science/nature/6170346.stm
A short article that gives an impression of the journey on board ship.

www.nmm.ac.uk/server/show/conWebDoc.142
Some basic information from the National Maritime Museum in London, UK, about Magellan's journey, with links to pages about life at sea in the past.

www.britannica.com/eb/article-9049979/Ferdinand-Magellan
Encyclopaedia Britannica article about Magellan's life and travels.

Places to Visit

The Mary Rose
The Mary Rose Trust, College Road, HM Naval Base, Portsmouth, Hants PO1 3LX
Museum tel 023 9281 2931

King Henry VIII's famous warship, which sank in 1545. Its remains were raised in 1982 and are now preserved in Portsmouth.

Cowes Maritime Museum
Beckford Road, Cowes, Isle of Wight PO31 7SG
Tel 01983 293394

All about the shipbuilding industry in the past.

Scottish Maritime Museum
Harbourside, Irvine KA12 8QE, Scotland
Tel 01294 278283

Shipbuilding in Scotland and collections of ships dating from the 18th century.

Index